The 30-Day Money Detox: Fix Your Financial Chaos

From Broke to Baseline in One Month

Niramaya Iyer

ISBN: 978-93-47365-67-6

First Edition

Title: The 30-Day Money Detox: Fix Your Financial Chaos
Subtitle: From Broke to Baseline in One Month
Author: Niramaya Iyer

Published by:
Divamani Enterprises
Ernakulam, India
Website: www.divamani.in
Email: divamani.enterprises@divamani.in

Contents

Your Wake-Up Call

It's the 18th of the month.

Priya opens her banking app with that familiar feeling in her stomach. You know the one – half dread, half resignation. She earned ₹75,000 last month. A good salary. But her balance shows ₹3,247.

Two weeks left until salary day.

She scrolls through recent transactions. ₹850 for coffee and snacks last week. ₹1,200 for those earrings she wore once. ₹2,400 on Swiggy because she was too tired to cook. ₹680 for that app subscription she forgot she had.

None of it feels like a big deal. But here she is. Again.

Sound familiar?

You make decent money. You're not reckless. You don't blow thousands on shopping sprees or expensive vacations. But somehow, every month, you're scraping by at the end. Checking your balance before every purchase. Avoiding that dinner invite because you're "saving money" (even though you can't explain where the money went).

Here's the truth: You're not bad with money. You're just in financial chaos.

And chaos has a pattern. It's not the big disasters that break you. It's the hundred small leaks you don't see. The invisible expenses. The emotional spending after a bad day. The subscriptions you forgot. The "just this once" purchases that happen three times a week.

That's why you picked up this book.

You're tired of the chaos. Tired of the dread. Tired of making good money and having nothing to show for it. You want control. You want to stop checking your bank balance with anxiety. You want to actually have money left at the end of the month instead of month left at the end of your money.

That's exactly what the next 30 days will give you.

This isn't about budgeting apps or investment strategies or becoming a millionaire. This is about going from financial chaos to financial baseline. From broke to stable. From dread to control.

Here's what the next month looks like:

Week 1: Reality Check – You'll track every rupee and discover exactly where your money goes. Not where you think it goes. Where it actually goes.

Week 2: Enemy Identification – You'll identify which psychological enemies are destroying your wallet. Ego? Envy? FOMO? Once you see them, you can fight them.

Week 3: Build the Fortress – You'll start your first emergency fund. Even ₹10,000 will change how you sleep at night.

Week 4: Plug the Leaks – You'll find and eliminate ₹3,000 to ₹8,000 per month in wasteful spending you didn't even know existed.

By Day 30, you'll have:

1. A starter emergency fund of ₹10,000-20,000
2. Complete awareness of every expense
3. Your primary financial enemy identified and managed
4. ₹3,000-8,000 in monthly expenses cut
5. A clear system for the next 60 days

Most importantly, you'll feel in control for the first time.

How to use this book

This is a workbook, not a novel. Each chapter gives you specific tasks for each day. Some take 10 minutes. Some take an hour. But every single one matters.

Track daily. Review weekly. Adjust constantly.

Don't skip days. Don't tell yourself "I'll do it later." The whole point is building momentum over 30 consecutive days. Miss a day, and you lose the compound effect.

You don't need to be perfect. You just need to be consistent.

Ready?

Let's start with the hardest part: Looking at the truth.

Week 1: Reality Check (Days 1-7)

Your Financial Snapshot

By the end of this chapter, you'll know your exact financial position – no more guessing.

Rahul thought he was doing fine.

Software engineer. ₹90,000 monthly salary. That's ₹550 per hour based on the standard 8-hour day, right?

Wrong.

When he actually tracked his work hours for a week – including the "quick" evening emails, weekend "urgent" fixes, and late-night deployments – he was working 12-hour days. Some days, 14 hours.

His real hourly rate? ₹225.

Not ₹550. Not even ₹300.

₹225 per hour for someone with five years of experience.

That ₹1050 he spent on a branded t-shirt? Nearly 5 hours of actual work. The reality hit him hard.

You can't fix what you don't measure. And you can't measure what you're avoiding.

Most people are avoiding the truth about their money.

They check their balance nervously but don't track expenses. They know their salary but not their real hourly rate. They have a vague sense of "owing money" but no clear picture of assets versus liabilities.

This week, we end the avoidance.

The next seven days will give you complete financial clarity. It won't all be comfortable. But it will be liberating.

Day 1-2: The Income Audit

Let's start with what's coming in.

Day 1 Task: List all your income sources

Write down every single source of money:

- Primary salary (post-tax, in-hand amount)
- Freelance or side gigs
- Rental income
- Interest or dividends
- Family support
- Anything else

Be specific. If your salary varies, take the average of the last three months.

Got it written down? Good.

Day 2 Task: Calculate your real hourly rate

Here's where it gets interesting.

Take your monthly in-hand salary. Divide it by the actual hours you work — not the official hours, the real hours. Include:

- Commute time (it's work-related, you can't use it for anything else)
- Unpaid overtime
- Checking work emails at night
- Weekend "quick tasks"

Rahul's calculation:

- Monthly salary: ₹90,000
- Official hours: 160 per month (8 hours × 20 working days)
- Actual hours: 400 per month (12-14 hour days + weekends) - Real hourly rate: ₹90,000 ÷ 400 = ₹225/hour

Why does this matter?

Because the next time you're about to spend ₹2,000 on something you don't need, you'll know that's 9 hours of your actual work. Suddenly, that impulse purchase feels different.

This is your wake-up call.

Write your real hourly rate on a sticky note. Put it where you'll see it daily. On your laptop. Your bathroom mirror. Anywhere you make spending decisions.

Day 3-4: The Expense Truth

Now for the hard part.

Most people think they know where their money goes. "Rent, food, transport, some shopping." Sounds reasonable.

Then they track it for a week and discover the truth.

Day 3 Task: Set up your expense tracking system

You have three options:

1. **Phone notes app** – Simple, always with you
2. **Spreadsheet** – Good for people who like organizing
3. **Expense tracking app** – Automated, categorizes for you

Pick one. Right now. Not later. Now.

For the next seven days, you will write down every single rupee you spend. Every. Single. One.

₹30 for chai? Write it down. ₹15 for parking? Write it down. ₹850 for groceries? Write it down. ₹1,200 on Swiggy? Write it down.

The rule: No transaction is too small to track.

Day 4 Task: Continue tracking + identify categories

By Day 4, you'll have about 48 hours of expenses tracked. Look at them. You'll start seeing patterns.

Create these categories:

- **Fixed Essentials** (rent, utilities, loan EMIs)
- **Variable Essentials** (groceries, transport, medicine)
- **Subscriptions** (Netflix, Spotify, gym, apps)
- **Food & Dining** (restaurants, delivery, coffee, snacks)

- **Shopping** (clothes, gadgets, accessories, random Amazon purchases)
- **Entertainment** (movies, events, hobbies)
- **Other** (everything else)

Start categorizing your expenses. This is where the invisible spending reveals itself.

Meera discovered she was spending ₹12,000 per month on food delivery. She knew she ordered Swiggy "sometimes." Turns out "sometimes" was 20 times a month. ₹600 average per order.

She wasn't eating at fancy restaurants. She was ordering "normal" food because she was tired after work. Each order felt small. ₹600 isn't a big deal, right?

But ₹600 × 20 times = ₹12,000.

That's the invisible expense. Death by a thousand cuts.

What are your invisible expenses?

You're about to find out.

Day 5-6: The Asset-Liability Check

Time to look at what you own versus what you owe.

Day 5 Task: List your assets

Assets are things that have value:

- Savings account balance
- Fixed deposits

- Investments (mutual funds, stocks, gold)
- Provident fund balance
- Any valuable items (laptop, phone if you can sell it, gold jewelry)

Write down the current value of each. Be honest. That laptop you bought for ₹85,000 three years ago? It's worth ₹25,000 now if you're lucky.

Add them up. That's your total assets.

Day 6 Task: List your liabilities

Liabilities are what you owe:

- Credit card outstanding (the full amount, not minimum due)
- Personal loans
- Car loan
- Education loan
- Money borrowed from family/friends

Write down each debt with:

- Total amount owed
- Interest rate
- Monthly payment

Add them up. That's your total liabilities.

Now calculate your net worth:

Net Worth = Total Assets - Total Liabilities

For many of you, this number will be negative. That's okay. You're not here to feel bad. You're here to fix it.

Amit's wake-up call:

- Assets: ₹45,000 (savings) + ₹80,000 (PF) = ₹1,25,000
- Liabilities: ₹2,40,000 (credit cards + personal loan)
- Net Worth: -₹1,15,000

He thought he was "doing okay." He had a job. He paid his bills (mostly). But on paper, he was more than a lakh in the hole.

Seeing the actual number changed everything.

What's your number?

Write it down. This is your starting point.

Day 7: Your Financial Dashboard

You've tracked expenses for 5 days. You know your real hourly rate. You know your net worth.

Time to create your dashboard – the three numbers you'll track every week from now on.

Your 3 Numbers:

1. **Monthly Income** (after tax, actual in-hand). Example: ₹75,000
2. **Monthly Expenses** (based on your 5-day tracking,extrapolated) Take your 5-day total, multiply by 6. Example: ₹18,000 in 5 days × 6 = ₹90,000 per month

3. **Net Worth** (assets minus liabilities). Example: -₹85,000

Look at numbers 1 and 2.

If your expenses are higher than your income, you're in a debt spiral. Every month, you're going backwards.

If they're about equal, you're on a treadmill. Running hard, going nowhere.

If your income is higher than expenses, you have room to build. But only if you stop the leaks.

Day 7 Task: Set up your weekly review ritual

Pick a day and time. Every week, same time. 30 minutes.

Sunday evening works for most people. Saturday morning if you prefer. Friday after work if that's your style.

Block it in your calendar right now. "Weekly Money Date."

During this 30 minutes, you'll:

- Review the week's expenses
- Update your dashboard
- Identify any unusual spending
- Plan the week ahead

This ritual is non-negotiable. Miss it, and the chaos creeps back in.

Case Study: Amit's Week 1

Amit, 28, software engineer, ₹85,000 monthly salary.

Before tracking:

- Thought he spent ₹60,000 per month
- Had "some" credit card debt
- Felt generally okay about his finances

After Week 1:

- Actual expenses: ₹92,000 per month
- Credit card debt: ₹2,40,000 at 42% interest
- Net worth: -₹1,15,000
- Invisible expenses discovered: ₹15,000/month (subscriptions, food delivery, impulse purchases he'd forgotten about)

The revelation: He was spending ₹7,000 more than he earned every month. For the past two years. That's where the credit card debt came from. Not one big purchase. A hundred small ones.

Seeing the actual numbers was brutal. But necessary.

Week 1 gave Amit clarity. The same clarity you now have.

Action Steps:

✓ Calculate your real hourly rate

✓ Track every single expense for 5 days minimum

✓ List all assets and liabilities

✓ Calculate your net worth

✓ Create your 3-number dashboard

✓ Schedule your weekly money review ritual

Key Takeaways:

- **You can't fix what you don't measure.** Financial chaos thrives in vagueness. Clarity kills it.
- **Most people underestimate expenses by 30-40%.** Your invisible spending is probably ₹10,000-15,000 per month.
- **Your real hourly rate changes how you think about spending.** That ₹2,000 impulse buy just became 11 hours of work.
- **Net worth is your true financial position.** Salary doesn't matter if debt is growing faster.
- **Awareness is the first step to control.** Now you see it. Next week, you'll understand why it happens.

Tomorrow, you'll meet the six enemies destroying your wallet.

Week 2: Enemy Identification (Days 8-14)

The Six Enemies Destroying Your Wallet

By the end of this chapter, you'll identify which enemy controls your spending and how to fight it.

Ananya is standing in Zara.

She doesn't need a handbag. She has four at home. But her colleague Neha just posted a photo on Instagram with this exact bag. ₹12,000. Limited edition.

Her hand hovers over her credit card.

"If Neha can afford it, why can't I? We have the same salary."

She buys it.

Two weeks later, she can't make her credit card minimum payment. She hasn't used the bag once. But every time she sees Neha, she feels that small win. "I have it too."

That's Envy. And it just cost Ananya ₹12,000 she didn't have.

Here's what nobody tells you about money: **Your financial problems are 80% psychology, 20% math.**

You know you shouldn't buy things you can't afford. You know subscriptions add up. You know credit card interest is brutal. You've heard it all before.

But you do it anyway.

Why?

Because six internal enemies are sabotaging you. They're subtle. They're convincing. And they speak in your own voice, so you think it's you making rational decisions.

It's not.

Let me introduce you to your enemies.

Day 8-9: Meet Your Enemies

These six enemies have been destroying wealth for thousands of years. They're psychological patterns that feel like common sense in the moment but create financial disasters over time.

Enemy #1: Greed

Greed isn't just wanting more. It's the "get rich quick" impulse. The shortcut addiction.

How it shows up:

- FOMO investing – "Everyone's making money in crypto, I can't miss out"
- Get-rich-quick schemes – "This course will teach me to make ₹1 lakh per month"
- Gambling disguised as investing – Putting money you can't afford to lose into volatile assets
- Overleveraging – Taking massive risk for massive (unlikely) reward

Karthik saw Bitcoin going up. Everyone in his office Slack was talking about it. He had ₹2 lakhs in savings.

He could have put ₹20,000 as a speculative bet. Instead, he put all ₹2 lakhs at the peak. Three months later, it was worth ₹75,000. He panic-sold.

Greed told him: "This is your chance to get ahead fast." Reality showed him: Slow and steady wasn't exciting, but it was working. Greed destroyed it.

Enemy #2: Anger

Anger spending is revenge against your own life.

How it shows up:

- Shopping after a bad day at work
- Expensive dinner because you "deserve it" after that client meeting
- Buying something nice for yourself because no one else appreciates you
- Stress shopping – the dopamine hit that makes you feel better for 20 minutes

Divya had a terrible boss. Every time she got yelled at in a meeting, she'd order something online during lunch. ₹800 here, ₹1,500 there, ₹3,000 for a dress she'd never wear.

"I deserve this. I work hard."

In six months, she accumulated ₹65,000 in credit card debt. The boss was still terrible. Now she also had debt stress.

Anger told her: "This will make you feel better." Reality showed her: Temporary relief, permanent damage.

Enemy #3: Arrogance

Arrogance is thinking you're the exception to the rules.

How it shows up:

- "I can handle this debt, I'll pay it off next month" (you won't)
- Ignoring credit card interest because "I'm smart about money"
- Taking a loan you can barely afford because "my salary will increase"
- Overleveraging on EMIs – "I can manage it"

Rohan bought a car with an EMI of ₹34,000 per month. His salary was ₹75,000. That's 45% of his income going to one asset that's depreciating.

When friends questioned it, he said: "I've budgeted for it. I'm disciplined."

Six months in, he missed a payment. Then another. His credit score tanked. When he needed a personal loan for a family emergency, he was rejected.

Arrogance told him: "You're smart enough to make this work." Reality showed him: Math doesn't care about your confidence.

Enemy #4: Delusion

Delusion is attachment to fantasy despite evidence.

How it shows up:

- "This time it's different" thinking
- Ignoring red flags in investments
- Believing your spending will magically decrease next month (it won't)
- Thinking you don't need an emergency fund because "nothing bad will happen to me"

Sneha kept saying she'd start saving "next month" for two years. This month was always tight because of "unexpected" expenses.

Except they weren't unexpected. Her friend's birthday. Diwali shopping. AC repair. Shoes wearing out. These things happen every year. They're not unexpected. They're unplanned.

She had no emergency fund. When her laptop died, she had to borrow ₹45,000 from her parents at age 29.

Delusion told her: "I'll start saving once things stabilize." Reality showed her: Things never stabilize. You create stability.

Enemy #5: Ego

Ego spending is paying for the image of success.

How it shows up:

- Status purchases – brands over utility
- Keeping up with friends who earn more than you
- Expensive restaurants not for the food but for the Instagram post
- Picking up the bill to look generous when you can't afford it

Rajesh always insisted on paying when out with friends. ₹3,500 dinners, ₹2,000 bar bills. He earned ₹60,000. His friends earned ₹1,20,000+.

They could afford it. He couldn't.

But the moment of "No, I've got this" felt good. People thought he was doing well. Nobody knew he was ₹1.8 lakhs in debt.

Ego told him: "This is what successful people do." Reality showed him: Appearing successful isn't the same as being successful.

Enemy #6: Envy

Envy is the comparison trap.

How it shows up:

- Buying because someone else has it
- Lifestyle matching people who earn more than you
- Upgrade pressure – your phone is fine, but your colleague got the new iPhone

- Feeling "behind" because of social media

Priya didn't care about expensive headphones. Then her colleague showed up with AirPods Pro. ₹25,000.

Suddenly, Priya's ₹1,500 headphones felt cheap. Within a week, she bought them too. On EMI. For headphones.

She still uses them. But they don't sound 16x better than her old ones. They just match her colleague's.

Envy told her: "If she can have nice things, you should too." Reality showed her: Her colleague doesn't have her student loans. Comparison is a trap.

Day 10-11: Your Primary Enemy

All six enemies will visit you. But one dominates.

Day 10 Task: Take the enemy quiz

For each enemy, rate 1-5 how often this shows up in your spending:

Greed:

- I've invested in something risky hoping to get rich quick
- I buy courses/schemes promising huge returns
- I take bigger risks than I can afford
- I feel like I'm missing out on "opportunities"

Anger:

- I shop after stressful days
- I buy things to feel better emotionally

- I make purchases to "treat myself" when upset
- Spending is how I cope with frustration

Arrogance:

- I take on debt I'm confident I can handle (but struggle with)
- I ignore warnings about financial risks
- I think rules apply to others, not me
- I overestimate my discipline

Delusion:

- I keep thinking "next month I'll save"
- I ignore obvious financial red flags
- I don't plan for predictable expenses
- I think I don't need an emergency fund

Ego:

- I buy brands to impress people
- I spend beyond my means to maintain an image
- I pick up bills to look successful
- I care a lot about what others think of my lifestyle

Envy:

- I buy things because others have them
- I compare my lifestyle to friends/colleagues

- Instagram makes me want to shop
- I upgrade things that work fine because someone else upgraded

Scoring:

- Add up the scores for each enemy
- Your highest score is your primary enemy
- Your second-highest is your secondary enemy

Day 11 Task: Understand your enemy's pattern

Look at your Week 1 expense tracking. Go through each non-essential purchase.

For each one, ask: **Which enemy was driving this?**

Ananya's audit:

- ₹12,000 handbag → Envy (colleague had it)
- ₹2,400 dress → Anger (bad day at work)
- ₹850 restaurant → Ego (wanted to impress date)
- ₹3,500 gadget → Greed (thought it would make her more productive/successful)

Pattern: Envy and Greed dominated. 80% of her wasteful spending came from these two.

What's your pattern?

Day 12-13: The Defense System

Now that you know your enemy, you can fight it.

Day 12 Task: The 24-Hour Rule

Starting today, implement this non-negotiable rule:

For any non-essential purchase over ₹500, wait 24 hours before buying.

Don't "think about it while shopping." Don't "add to cart and decide later."

Physically leave. If online, close the tab.

24 hours later, if you still want it and can afford it, buy it.

Here's what happens in those 24 hours:

The emotional spike flattens. The dopamine hit fades. You see the purchase clearly instead of through the enemy's lens.

Studies show the 24-hour rule stops 60% of impulse purchases. Just by waiting.

For purchases over ₹5,000, make it 72 hours. For purchases over ₹20,000, make it one week.

Day 13 Task: Identify your triggers

Your enemies don't attack randomly. They have triggers.

Common triggers:

- Scrolling Instagram (Envy)
- Bad day at work (Anger)
- Friends talking about investments (Greed, FOMO)
- Being in a mall/shopping area (multiple)

- Seeing someone else's success (Envy, Ego)
- Feeling insecure (Ego, Delusion)

Write down:

1. **When** you're most vulnerable (time of day, day of week)
2. **Where** enemy spending happens (online? specific stores? with certain people?)
3. **What** emotional state triggers it (stressed? bored? comparing yourself?)

Create defense rules:

- If Instagram triggers Envy → Limit to 15 minutes per day
- If malls trigger impulse buying → Don't browse, only shop with a list
- If stress triggers spending → Alternative coping (walk, call a friend, workout)
- If friends trigger FOMO → Be honest: "I'm on a financial detox this month"

Day 14: Weekly Review + Enemy Journal

Day 14 Task: Review Week 2 through the enemy lens

Pull up your expense tracking for Days 8-14.

For every purchase over ₹200, write:

- Amount
- What you bought

- Which enemy drove it (be honest)
- Could you have avoided it?

This isn't about guilt. It's about pattern recognition.

Karthik's revelation: 8 purchases in Week 2. 6 were Greed-driven (courses, "investment" opportunities, gadgets that promised productivity). Total: ₹18,000.

Now he knew: His primary enemy was Greed. And it was costing him ₹18,000 per week.

Start your Enemy Journal:

Create a simple note on your phone. Title: "Enemy Watch"

Every time you're about to make a purchase, write:

- What I want to buy
- Why I want it (actual reason, not justification)
- Which enemy is talking
- Decision: Buy / Wait / Skip

This five-second pause is a circuit breaker. It stops automatic spending.

Case Studies:

Karthik's Greed:

- Lost ₹2 lakhs in crypto FOMO
- Bought 3 courses (₹45,000 total) he never finished
- Constantly chasing "the next big thing"

- **After enemy identification:** Set rule — no investment decision without 72-hour wait + written research. Stopped impulsive "opportunities."

Divya's Anger:

- ₹65,000 credit card debt from stress shopping
- Every bad day at work = online purchase
- Retail therapy became retail damage
- **After enemy identification:** New rule — bad days mean gym or call a friend, not shopping. Alternative dopamine sources.

Rohan's Ego:

- ₹34,000 car EMI he couldn't afford (45% of income)
- Bought to match colleague's lifestyle
- Status over stability
- **After enemy identification:** Sold car, bought used one, EMI dropped to ₹12,000. Pride hurt for a month. Finances recovered for years.

Action Steps:

✓ Take the enemy identification quiz

✓ Identify your primary and secondary enemies

✓ Review Week 1 expenses through the enemy lens

✓ Implement the 24-hour rule for purchases over ₹500

✓ List your personal spending triggers

✓ Create defense rules for each trigger

✓ Start your Enemy Journal

Key Takeaways:

- **Financial problems are 80% psychology, 20% math.** Your enemies sabotage you more than lack of knowledge.
- **Everyone has a primary enemy.** Knowing yours gives you power. You can't fight what you can't see.
- **The 24-hour rule stops 60% of impulse purchases.** Just by creating space between wanting and buying.
- **Triggers are predictable.** Once you know when/where/why you overspend, you can create defenses.
- **Awareness breaks the automatic pattern.** The Enemy Journal gives you a circuit breaker.

Next week, you'll build your fortress: The emergency fund that changes everything.

Week 3: Build the Fortress (Days 15-21)

Your First Emergency Fund

By the end of this chapter, you'll have started your emergency fund and know exactly how to build it to ₹50,000 in 90 days.

May in Delhi. 42 degrees outside.

Vikram's AC stops working.

The repair guy comes. Motor burned out. ₹18,000 to fix.

Vikram checks his bank account. ₹4,200.

Checks his savings. ₹0. (He was going to start saving "next month.")

He pulls out his credit card. 42% annual interest. But what choice does he have?

₹18,000 becomes ₹20,655 after interest. He takes four months to pay it off. An ₹18,000 emergency just cost him ₹20,655 because he had no emergency fund.

Without an emergency fund, every crisis becomes a debt trap.

This week, that changes.

Day 15-16: Why Emergency Funds Are Non-Negotiable

Let's talk about the modern Indian reality.

Job volatility: Companies downsize. Startups fold. Even stable jobs aren't guaranteed. The average person changes jobs 7-10 times in their career. Some of those transitions aren't planned.

Family emergencies: Your parents need medical care. Your sibling needs financial help. These aren't possibilities. They're certainties. The only question is when.

Health crises: Medical insurance is great. Until you discover it doesn't cover everything. Co-pays, deductibles, treatments "not covered" – they add up fast.

Unexpected repairs: AC breaks. Laptop dies. Phone cracks. Car needs repair. These aren't disasters, but without funds, they create disaster-level stress.

The ancient principle: In classical Indian texts, rulers were advised to maintain a **Kosha** – a treasury specifically for calamities and uncertainties. Not for expansion. Not for glory. For survival when things go wrong.

You need a personal Kosha.

Day 15 Task: Calculate the cost of not having emergency funds

Think back over the past year.

List every unexpected expense that stressed you out:

- Medical bills
- Repairs (phone, laptop, vehicle, home)
- Family emergencies

- Job loss or income gap
- Any other surprise expense

For each one, write:

- What you paid
- How you paid (savings, credit card, borrowing)
- If you paid interest/borrowed, what the true cost was

Meera's list:

- Father's hospital co-pay: ₹45,000 (credit card, paid ₹52,000 after interest)
- Laptop replacement: ₹60,000 (borrowed from friend, strained relationship)
- Scooter repair: ₹8,500 (credit card)
- Emergency flight home: ₹12,000 (delayed paying rent)

Total emergency costs: ₹1,25,500

True cost with interest/stress: ₹1,47,000+

If she'd had a ₹50,000 emergency fund, she could have:

- Handled three of these without debt
- Reduced stress by 80%
- Saved ₹21,500 in interest alone

Day 16 Task: Understand what emergency funds do

An emergency fund isn't just money. It's three things:

1. **A financial airbag** You hope you never crash. But if you do, it saves your life. Same with emergency funds.
2. **Decision-making power** Suresh got laid off. He had four months of expenses saved. He could wait for the right job instead of desperately taking the first offer. That patience got him 30% higher salary than his previous job.

   No emergency fund? You take the first offer out of panic. Desperation kills negotiation power.
3. **Stress elimination** The greatest gift isn't the money. It's sleeping well. Not panicking when the check engine light comes on. Not checking your credit card limit before calling the plumber.

   Financial stress is constant, low-grade anxiety. An emergency fund kills it.

Day 17-18: Your Target Number

Let's be realistic. You're reading this book because you're in financial chaos. I'm not going to tell you to save ₹5 lakhs immediately.

We're building in stages.

The Build-Up Plan:

Stage 1: Starter Fund (30 days) → ₹10,000

Covers small emergencies: Minor medical, phone repair, small unexpected bills

Goal: Complete by Day 30 of this detox

Stage 2: Basic Security (90 days) → ₹50,000

Covers: Major repairs, moderate medical, 1-month essential expenses

Goal: Complete by Day 90 (two months after this detox ends)

Stage 3: Full Fortress (6-12 months) → 6 months of essential expenses

Covers: Job loss, major medical, extended crisis

Goal: Build over time, starting from Day 91

Day 17 Task: Calculate YOUR 6-month target

This is your ultimate emergency fund goal. Don't panic – you're not building this in 30 days. But you need to know the target.

Step 1: Calculate monthly essential expenses

From your Week 1 tracking, list only essentials:

- Rent/mortgage
- Utilities (electricity, water, internet)
- Groceries (basic, not dining out)
- Transport (minimal)
- Insurance premiums
- Loan EMIs (can't skip these)
- Medicine (if ongoing)

Priya's essentials:

- Rent: ₹15,000
- Utilities: ₹2,500
- Groceries: ₹6,000
- Transport: ₹2,000
- Insurance: ₹1,500
- EMI: ₹8,000
- **Total per month: ₹35,000**

Step 2: Multiply by 6

Priya's 6-month target: ₹35,000 × 6 = **₹2,10,000**

That's her Full Fortress number. Seems huge, right?

It is. That's why we're not starting there.

Day 18 Task: Set your 30-day realistic goal

Based on your income and current expenses, what can you save in 30 days?

Be aggressive but realistic.

If you earn ₹40,000-60,000: Target ₹8,000-12,000

If you earn ₹60,000-1,00,000: Target ₹12,000-20,000

If you earn ₹1,00,000+: Target ₹20,000-30,000

These assume you've already cut wasteful spending in Weeks 1-2.

Write your 30-day target: ₹ ____________

This is the number you'll hit by Day 30.

Day 19-20: Where to Keep It

You've decided to build an emergency fund. Where does the money go?

Day 19 Task: Set up your Kosha account

Rule #1: Separate account

Do NOT keep your emergency fund in your salary account.

Why? Psychology.

If it's in your main account, you'll see the balance and think "I have money, I can spend." The mental accounting gets blurred.

Separate account = separate mental category = much harder to touch impulsively.

Where to open it:

Option 1: High-interest savings account

- Look for 6-7% interest
- Zero or low minimum balance
- Easy transfer but not instant (small friction is good)
- Examples: Digital banks often have higher rates

Option 2: Liquid mutual fund

- 6-8% returns
- Can withdraw in 24 hours (T+1 day)
- Slightly better returns than savings account

- Small friction prevents impulse dipping

Option 3: Sweep-in Fixed Deposit

- Linked to savings account
- Earns FD rates when balance crosses threshold
- Auto-breaks when you need money
- Good option if your bank offers it

What NOT to use:

✗ **Stocks or equity mutual funds** – Can crash 30% right when you need the money

✗ **Crypto** – Volatility will destroy you in emergencies

✗ **Locked FDs** – Can't access quickly, defeats the purpose

✗ **Your main salary account** – Too easy to accidentally spend

Day 20 Task: Set it up TODAY

Not tomorrow. Not next week. Today.

Go online. Open a separate savings account or liquid fund. Right now.

It takes 15 minutes. There's no reason to delay except avoidance.

Once it's set up, name it. "Emergency Fund" or "Kosha" or "Fortress" or "My Financial Airbag."

Make it real.

Day 21: First Transfer

This is the most important day of Week 3.

Day 21 Task: Make your first deposit

Transfer money into your Kosha account TODAY.

Even if it's just ₹1,000. Even if it's ₹500.

The amount matters less than the action.

Why?

Because **starting creates momentum.** Once there's money in that account, you want to see it grow. It becomes real. It becomes a priority.

If the account stays at zero, it's theoretical. Intentions don't build emergency funds. Deposits do.

How much to transfer today:

Look at your account balance. After covering this week's essential expenses, how much can you safely move?

₹2,000? Do it. ₹5,000? Do it. ₹500? Still worth it.

Then set up automation.

Automate your Kosha contributions:

The best method: Auto-transfer on salary day

Set up an automatic transfer for the day after your salary hits.

If you earn ₹75,000 and want to save ₹15,000 this month:

- Day 1 (salary day): ₹75,000 arrives
- Day 2 (auto-transfer): ₹15,000 moves to Kosha
- Day 2 onwards: You live on ₹60,000

Why Day 2, not Day 5 or Day 10?

Because by Day 5, you'll have spent it. "I'll transfer after I pay these bills" turns into "I'll do it next month."

Pay yourself first. Automate it. Remove the decision.

Alternative if salary varies:

Set up a weekly auto-transfer. Every Monday, ₹2,000 moves to Kosha. By month-end, you've saved ₹8,000+ without thinking about it.

The rule: Out of sight, out of mind, into the fortress.

Case Studies:

Meera's Medical Emergency: Had ₹1.5 lakh emergency fund when father needed surgery. Insurance covered 80%. She paid ₹45,000 from Kosha without stress or debt. Rebuilt fund over next 6 months.

Suresh's Job Loss: Lost job unexpectedly. Had 4-month Kosha. Didn't panic. Took time to interview properly. Got offer 30% higher than previous job. Emergency fund = negotiation power.

Pradeep's Mistake: Kept "emergency fund" in stock investments. Needed ₹60,000 for urgent repair. Market was down 25%. Had to sell at a loss. Lost ₹15,000 because of wrong vehicle.

The lesson: Liquidity matters more than returns for emergency funds.

Action Steps:

✓ Calculate what your lack of emergency fund has cost you in the past year

✓ Understand the three functions of an emergency fund

✓ Calculate your 6-month Full Fortress target

✓ Set your realistic 30-day goal (₹8,000-20,000)

✓ Open a separate Kosha account (savings or liquid fund)

✓ Make your first deposit TODAY (any amount)

✓ Set up automatic transfers on salary day

Key Takeaways:

- **Emergency funds are financial airbags.** You hope you never crash, but they save your life when you do.
- **Start small: ₹10,000 in 30 days is achievable.** Don't get paralyzed by the big number. Build in stages.
- **Separate account = separate mental category.** Psychology matters more than interest rates for emergency funds.
- **Automate on salary day.** Pay yourself first, or you'll never pay yourself at all.
- **Liquidity > Returns.** Emergency funds should be boring and accessible, not volatile and high-return.

Next week, you'll find the money to fill your Kosha faster: Plug the invisible leaks.

Week 4: Plug the Leaks (Days 22-28)

Stop the Invisible Money Drain

By the end of this chapter, you'll have identified and eliminated ₹3,000-8,000/month in wasteful spending.

Sneha got a ₹15,000 raise. From ₹60,000 to ₹75,000 per month.

Finally, she'd be able to save. The extra ₹15,000 would go straight into investments.

Six months later, she's more broke than before.

Where did the ₹15,000 go?

She has no idea. It just... disappeared.

This is **lifestyle inflation.** And it's silent, invisible, and deadly to your finances.

Day 22-23: The Lifestyle Inflation Trap

Here's how lifestyle inflation works:

You get a raise. You feel like you can afford slightly nicer things. None of them are dramatic.

You upgrade from bus to cab a few days a week. "I'm tired, I deserve it."

You order food delivery more often. "I'm earning more, why should I cook when I'm exhausted?"

You add a subscription or two. "It's just ₹500 per month."

You go from two restaurant meals per month to five. "I can afford to enjoy life now."

Individually, each decision makes sense. Collectively, they eat your entire raise.

Day 22 Task: The raise autopsy

Think back to your last salary increase. (If you haven't had one, think about the difference between what you earn now versus two years ago.)

Write down:

- Your old salary
- Your new salary
- The difference (your "raise")

Now list what upgraded in your lifestyle since then:

- More food delivery?
- Better phone plan?
- More expensive clothes?
- Nicer restaurants?
- Additional subscriptions?
- More cabs, less public transport?
- Bigger apartment?

Calculate the monthly cost of each upgrade.

Sneha's autopsy:

Raise: ₹15,000/month - Upgrades:

- Food delivery 2x/week → 6x/week: +₹6,000/month
- Switched to unlimited data plan: +₹500/month

- Added gym membership (doesn't use): +₹2,000/month
- Restaurants 2x/month → 8x/month: +₹4,000/month
- Cab to work 2x/week (was always bus): +₹3,200/month
- New subscription services: +₹800/month

Total lifestyle inflation: ₹16,500

Her raise was ₹15,000. Lifestyle inflation was ₹16,500.

She went backwards.

Day 23 Task: Identify your personal inflation points

These are the areas where "temporary" upgrades became permanent:

Common inflation points:

- **Transport:** "I'll cab today, I'm tired" → Every day
- **Food:** "I'll order today, no time to cook" → Default mode
- **Subscriptions:** Added services you forgot you're paying for
- **Shopping frequency:** "Sometimes" became "often"
- **Brand upgrades:** ₹1,000 jeans became ₹4,000 jeans "because quality"

Review your Week 1-3 expense tracking. Compare current spending to six months ago (check old bank statements if needed).

Where did you inflate?

Day 24-25: The Subscription Audit

Subscriptions are the silent killers.

They're small enough to ignore individually. Large enough to destroy you collectively.

Day 24 Task: List EVERY subscription you're paying for

And I mean every single one:

Digital Entertainment:

- Netflix
- Amazon Prime
- Disney+ Hotstar
- Spotify
- YouTube Premium
- Other OTT platforms

Productivity & Software:

- Cloud storage (Google One, iCloud, Dropbox)
- Software subscriptions (Adobe, Microsoft, etc.)
- App subscriptions (meditation, fitness, productivity)

Physical Memberships:

- Gym
- Club memberships
- Magazine subscriptions
- Milk delivery
- Grocery subscriptions

Financial & Services:

- Premium banking services
- Credit card annual fees
- App-based services (dating apps, premium features)

The ones you forgot:

- Check your bank/card statements for recurring charges
- Look for that ₹99, ₹199, ₹499 charge every month
- Those add up

Day 25 Task: The brutal math

For each subscription, calculate:

1. Monthly cost
2. Annual cost (monthly × 12)
3. When you last used it meaningfully?
4. Can you get it free or cheaper?

Kavya's audit:

Subscription	Monthly	Annual	Last Used
Netflix	₹649	₹7,788	Yesterday
Amazon Prime (annual package)	₹125	₹1,499	Last week
Hotstar	₹299	₹3,588	3 months ago
Spotify	₹119	₹1,428	Daily
YouTube Premium	₹129	₹1,548	Never (free trial ended, forgot to cancel)
Gym	₹2,000	₹24,000	4 months ago
Cloud storage	₹130	₹1,560	Don't know
Meditation app	₹500	₹6,000	6 months ago

Subscription	Monthly	Annual	Last Used
Premium LinkedIn	₹1,600	₹19,200	Once

Total: ₹5,551 /month = ₹66,611/year

The brutal questions:

For each subscription, ask:

1. **Would I re-subscribe to this today if I had to make the decision fresh?**
2. **Am I getting ₹X worth of value per month?**
3. **Can I downgrade to a cheaper tier?**
4. **Can I share with someone to split the cost?**

Kavya's decisions:

- Keep Netflix (uses it)
- Keep Amazon Prime (uses it)
- **Cancel Hotstar** (hasn't used in months) → Save ₹3,588/year
- Keep Spotify (daily use)
- **Cancel YouTube Premium** (forgot she had it) → Save ₹1,548/year
- **Cancel gym** (hasn't gone, can workout at home) → Save ₹24,000/year
- **Downgrade cloud storage** (using 20% of capacity) → Save ₹780/year

- **Cancel meditation app** (can use free alternatives) → Save ₹6,000/year
- **Cancel LinkedIn Premium** (not using) → Save ₹19,200/year

Total saved: ₹55,116 per year = ₹4,593 per month

By spending 30 minutes canceling subscriptions, Kavya freed up ₹4,593 every month. For doing nothing. Just stopping payments for things she wasn't using.

Your turn. Cancel at least 3 subscriptions this week.

Day 26-27: Infrastructure vs. Luxury Framework

Not all spending is equal. Some builds capacity. Some just feels good temporarily.

Day 26 Task: Learn the framework

Infrastructure spending:

- Builds long-term capacity
- Saves time or creates time
- Protects health
- Generates value or income
- Appreciates or holds value

Examples:

- Good internet (enables work from home, saves commute)
- Quality shoes (protects health, lasts longer)

- Books/courses that build real skills (increases earning potential)
- Ergonomic chair (prevents back problems)
- Durable basics (saves replacement costs)

Luxury spending:

- Temporary pleasure
- Status-driven
- Depreciating rapidly
- Doesn't build capacity
- Could get same function cheaper

Examples:

- Expensive branded clothes for the logo (₹5,000 shirt vs. ₹800 equivalent)
- Latest phone when current one works fine
- Daily cabs when bus/metro works
- Restaurant meals for convenience, not experience
- Gadgets you'll use once

The test: Infrastructure or Luxury?

Ask yourself:

1. **Will this save me time/money in the long run?**
2. **Does this build capacity or just signal status?**
3. **Am I buying function or brand?**
4. **Will I get value from this in 6 months?**

Day 27 Task: Audit this week's expenses

Go through Days 22-27 spending. For each purchase over ₹200, categorize:

- Infrastructure
- Luxury
- Unclear

Be honest.

Arjun's audit:

- ₹3,500 on restaurant meal → **Luxury** (could have cooked)
- ₹1,200 on running shoes → **Infrastructure** (health, will last 2 years)
- ₹2,800 on productivity course → **Unclear** → Will I actually finish it? (If yes, Infrastructure. If no, Luxury)
- ₹4,500 on branded shirt → **Luxury** (₹1,200 shirt would function the same)

The insight:

You don't need to cut all luxury. Life needs some pleasure.

But **conscious luxury** is choosing what genuinely matters to you and cutting the rest.

Arjun loves good coffee. That's his luxury. He'll pay ₹200 for specialty coffee and enjoy every sip.

But he doesn't care about branded clothes. So he stopped buying them.

That's the difference between deprivation and optimization.

Day 28: The "Worth It" List

Final day of Week 4. Time to get clear on your values.

Day 28 Task: Create your "Worth It" list

This is personal. No judgment. Just honesty.

Part 1: Things you'll NEVER cut

List 5-10 expenses that genuinely bring you joy or value:

- These might be "luxuries" but they're YOUR luxuries
- They're conscious, intentional, worth the money
- Cutting them would make you miserable

Tanvi's "Worth It" list:

1. Monthly book budget (₹1,500)
2. Coffee with friends twice a month (₹1,200)
3. Annual vacation (₹30,000 saved over 12 months)
4. Gym membership I actually use (₹1,800)
5. Quality skincare (₹2,000/month)

Total: ₹6,500/month + vacation savings

She values these. They're staying.

Part 2: Things you'll cut guilt-free

List 5-10 expenses you don't actually care about:

- You do them out of habit or social pressure
- They don't bring real joy
- You won't miss them

Tanvi's "Cut" list:

1. Restaurant meals for convenience (not special occasions) → Cook instead
2. Brand clothes for logos → Buy unbranded equivalents
3. Unused subscriptions → Already cancelled
4. Daily cab to work → Switch to metro (save ₹4,000/month)
5. Impulse online shopping → 24-hour rule prevents this

Total saved: ₹8,000+/month

The magic:

Tanvi didn't cut her "worth it" spending. She still has her books, her coffee dates, her skincare.

But she cut ₹8,000/month in things she doesn't care about.

That's **conscious spending.** Spending on what matters. Cutting what doesn't.

Your "Worth It" list (max 10 items):

1. ___
2. ___
3. ___
4. ___
5. ___
6. ___
7. ___
8. ___
9. ___

10. ___

Everything else is negotiable.

Case Studies:

Kavya's Subscription Audit: Cut ₹4,593/month in subscriptions she wasn't using. That's ₹55,116/year. In 30 minutes. Zero lifestyle impact. Just stopped paying for forgotten services.

Tanvi's Dining Strategy: Was eating out 12 times a month (₹18,000). Didn't enjoy most of them – just convenience. Cut to 4 special meals per month (₹8,000). Enjoyed them MORE because they were intentional. Saved ₹10,000/month.

Arjun's Raise Strategy: Got ₹20,000 raise. Before lifestyle inflation could eat it:

- 50% to emergency fund (₹10,000)
- 30% for quality-of-life upgrades (₹6,000)
- 20% for guilt-free enjoyment (₹4,000)

Pre-decided allocation prevented invisible spending. He actually felt the raise instead of wondering where it went.

Action Steps:

✓ Conduct your raise autopsy (where did lifestyle inflate?)

✓ List every single subscription you're paying for

✓ Calculate annual cost of subscriptions

✓ Cancel at least 3 this week

✓ Learn Infrastructure vs. Luxury framework

✓ Audit this week's expenses: Infrastructure or Luxury?

✓ Create your "Worth It" list (max 10 items)

✓ Identify ₹5,000+/month to redirect to emergency fund

Key Takeaways:

- **The average person has 7-12 subscriptions, uses 3-4.** That's ₹2,000-5,000/month in waste.
- **Lifestyle inflation is silent.** Raises disappear into tiny upgrades you don't consciously decide to keep.
- **Spending on what you love ≠ spending on everything.** Conscious spending means keeping your "worth it" items and cutting the rest.
- **Infrastructure builds capacity. Luxury signals status.** Know which is which.
- **The 24-hour rule + "Worth It" list = 70% reduction in wasteful spending.** Simple systems, massive impact.

Next week: Lock it in. Measure your progress. Plan your next 60 days.

Week 5: Lock It In (Days 29-30 + Beyond)

Your 30-Day Scorecard & Next Steps

By the end of this chapter, you'll measure your progress and have a clear 60-day and 90-day plan.

Remember Priya?

Day 1. ₹3,000 left for two weeks. Opening her banking app with dread. The familiar anxiety.

Day 30. She opens her banking app.

Main account: ₹8,400

Emergency fund account: ₹18,000

She cancelled ₹3,800/month in subscriptions she wasn't using.

She identified her primary enemy (Envy – comparison shopping on Instagram).

She knows exactly where every rupee goes.

For the first time in years, she feels in control.

This can be you. This IS you if you've done the work.

Day 29: The 30-Day Assessment

Time to measure.

Day 29 Task: Compare starting point to today

Pull out your Week 1 data. Your Day 1 snapshot.

Then:

- Net worth: ₹________
- Monthly expenses: ₹________
- Emergency fund: ₹________
- Awareness level: Low/None
- Emotional state: Dread, anxiety, avoidance

Now (Day 29):

- Net worth: ₹________
- Monthly expenses: ₹________
- Emergency fund: ₹________
- Awareness level: High – you know where every rupee goes
- Emotional state: Control, clarity, confidence

Calculate the changes:

1. **Emergency Fund Progress**

   Target was ₹10,000-20,000. Where are you?

   If you hit ₹10,000+: **You succeeded.** You built a financial airbag from nothing in 30 days.

   If you hit ₹5,000-10,000: **You're close.** One more week and you're there. Don't stop now.

   If you hit less than ₹5,000: **You started.** That's more than 95% of people. Keep going.

2. **Monthly Expense Reduction**

   Compare Week 1 average weekly expenses to Week 4.

   Week 1 weekly average: ₹________ per month

   Week 4 weekly average: ₹________ per month

   Difference: ₹________

   Target was ₹3,000-8,000 reduction. How'd you do?

   Most people find ₹4,000-6,000 in cuts just from subscriptions and invisible spending.

3. **Awareness Level**

   Week 1: You guessed where money went. Probably underestimated by 30%.

   Week 4: You know every expense. No more surprises.

   This is worth more than the money saved. Awareness is control.

4. **Net Worth Change**

   Week 1 net worth: ₹________

   Week 4 net worth: ₹________

   Change: ₹________

   Even if it's still negative, it probably improved. Every rupee in emergency fund + every rupee of debt not added = net worth increase.

   Amit's 30-day change:

   - Started: -₹1,15,000 net worth

- Ended: -₹97,000 net worth
- Improvement: ₹18,000

Still negative. But moving in the right direction. For the first time in two years.

5. **Emotional State**

   This one's not measured in rupees.

   Do you still dread checking your bank balance?

   Or do you feel in control?

   Priya: "I used to avoid my banking app. Now I check it every day. Not out of fear. Out of curiosity. It's tracking progress instead of tracking disaster."

Day 30: The Next 60 Days

You've completed the detox. The chaos is gone. You have a baseline.

Now what?

Day 30 Task: Set your 60-day and 90-day goals

Days 31-60 Goals:

1. **Emergency Fund: ₹10,000 → ₹30,000**

   You've proven you can save. Now scale it.

   If you saved ₹10,000 in the first 30 days, you can save another ₹20,000 in the next 60.

   How:

   - Continue automated transfers on salary day

- Any bonuses, tax refunds, unexpected income → 100% to emergency fund
- Keep subscription cuts permanent (that's ₹3,000-5,000/month freed up)
- Apply the 24-hour rule (stops another ₹2,000-4,000/month in impulse spending)

2. **Implement 50/30/20 Rule**

   Now that you have expense awareness, structure your spending:

   - **50% Needs:** Rent, utilities, groceries, transport, insurance, EMIs
   - **30% Wants:** Dining out, entertainment, hobbies, "worth it" spending
   - **20% Savings/Debt:** Emergency fund, investments, extra debt payments

   If you earn ₹75,000:
   - Needs: ₹37,500
   - Wants: ₹22,500
   - Savings: ₹15,000

   Adjust percentages based on your situation. If you're in debt, maybe 50/20/30 (more to savings/debt payoff).

3. **Maintain Enemy Awareness**

   Your primary enemy doesn't disappear. It evolves.

   Keep the Enemy Journal for another 60 days. Every purchase over ₹500, note which enemy was involved.

Patterns will emerge. You'll get better at catching yourself.

Days 61-90 Goals:

1. **Emergency Fund: ₹30,000 → ₹50,000**

   By Day 90, you hit Basic Security level. ₹50,000 handles most emergencies without debt.

2. **Set Up Investment Automation**

   Once you have ₹50,000 emergency fund, start building wealth.

   Start small: ₹2,000-5,000/month.

   This isn't a get-rich-quick scheme. It's steady wealth building.

3. **Quarterly Financial Audit**

   Day 90 = End of Quarter 1.
   Review:

   - Net worth change (hopefully ₹50,000+ improvement)
   - Expense patterns (any lifestyle inflation creeping back?)
   - Enemy activity (which one is most active recently?)
   - Next quarter goals

The Maintenance System

Detoxes don't work if you go back to old habits on Day 31.

You need a maintenance system.

Weekly Money Date (30 minutes)

Every week, same day, same time.

What you do:

1. Review the week's expenses (10 minutes)
2. Categorize anything unusual (5 minutes)
3. Update your 3-number dashboard (5 minutes)
4. Check enemy journal: any patterns? (5 minutes)
5. Plan the week ahead: any expected large expenses? (5 minutes)

This 30-minute ritual prevents chaos from creeping back.

Monthly Net Worth Tracking

First Sunday of every month.

Calculate:

- Total assets (savings + investments + PF + valuables)
- Total liabilities (all debts)
- Net worth

Track it in a simple spreadsheet.

Watch the number go up. That's your scoreboard.

Quarterly Financial Audit

Every 90 days.

Deep review:

- Are expenses inflating? (Compare to 3 months ago)
- Is emergency fund on track?

- Any new enemies showing up?
- Are you still cutting wasteful spending?
- Time to increase contributions to savings?

Quarterly check-ins catch problems before they become crises.

Case Study: Where Are They Now?

Amit (Started: -₹1,15,000 net worth, ₹15,000/month invisible spending)

- Day 30: ₹12,000 emergency fund, cut ₹8,000/month in wasteful spending
- Day 90: ₹48,000 emergency fund, -₹89,000 net worth (paid down ₹26,000 in debt)
- Still has debt. But moving forward instead of backwards.

Karthik (Started: Greed-driven, lost ₹2 lakhs in crypto FOMO)

- Day 30: No new FOMO investments, ₹15,000 emergency fund started
- Day 90: ₹45,000 emergency fund, started ₹3,000/month SIP in boring index fund
- Learned: Slow beats zero. Steady beats desperate.

Priya (Started: ₹3,000 for 2 weeks, constant anxiety)

- Day 30: ₹18,000 emergency fund, ₹3,800/month subscription cuts

- Day 90: ₹52,000 emergency fund, sleeps well for first time in years
- Quote: "I'm not rich. But I'm not scared anymore."

Meera (Started: No emergency fund, borrowed ₹45,000 from parents)

- Day 30: ₹14,000 emergency fund
- Day 90: ₹50,000 emergency fund, repaid parents, started saving
- When her phone broke (₹18,000 replacement), she paid cash. No stress. No debt.

These are normal people. With normal salaries. Who did the work.

You can too.

Action Steps:

✓ Complete your 30-day self-assessment

✓ Measure: Emergency fund, expense reduction, net worth change

✓ Celebrate your wins (You've earned it. Acknowledge the progress.)

✓ Set 60-day targets (₹30,000 emergency fund + 50/30/20 implementation)

✓ Set 90-day targets (₹50,000 emergency fund + investment automation)

✓ Schedule weekly money dates for next month

Key Takeaways:

- **30 days of awareness creates habits that last.** The tracking, the enemy journal, the weekly reviews – these are now part of your system.
- **You don't need to be perfect, just consistent.** You'll slip. You'll have bad weeks. That's fine. The system catches you.
- **This is the foundation. Build on it in the next 60 days.** Chaos → Baseline → Stability → Growth. You're at Baseline. Next is Stability.
- **Emergency funds change everything.** Not just financially. Psychologically. Confidence replaces dread.
- **The work doesn't stop on Day 31.** Maintenance systems prevent backsliding. Weekly dates, monthly tracking, quarterly audits.

Final Thought

Thirty days ago, you were in financial chaos.

Today, you have clarity, control, and a growing emergency fund.

You know your enemies. You've plugged the leaks. You've built a fortress.

This isn't the end. This is the baseline.

The foundation is solid. Now you build.

See you in Book 2.

What's Next?

You've fixed the chaos. That was Book 1.

But there's more to financial health than "not broke."

Book 1: The 30-Day Money Detox ✓
You learnt to:

- Fix the chaos
- Build awareness
- Create emergency fund

Book 2: Stop the Bleed – Lifestyle Inflation & FOMO
You'll learn:

- How to handle salary increases without lifestyle creep
- The psychology of "deserving" purchases
- Building a spending system that scales with income
- Advanced enemy management (they evolve)
- Increasing savings rate from 15% to 40%

Who it's for: You've completed the 30-day detox. You have awareness and emergency fund started. Now you're ready to optimize and scale without backsliding.

Book 3: The Autopilot Wealth System
You'll learn:

- Investment automation that runs itself
- Building passive income streams
- Asset allocation by life stage
- The 10-year wealth blueprint

Who it's for: You've mastered spending. Emergency fund is solid. Now you're ready to build wealth that compounds while you focus on life.

You've completed the foundation. Everything else builds on this.

Welcome to financial control.

www.ingramcontent.com/pod-product-compliance
Lightning Source LLC
Chambersburg PA
CBHW011803160726
48282CB00035B/1244
* 9 7 8 9 3 4 7 3 6 5 6 7 6 *